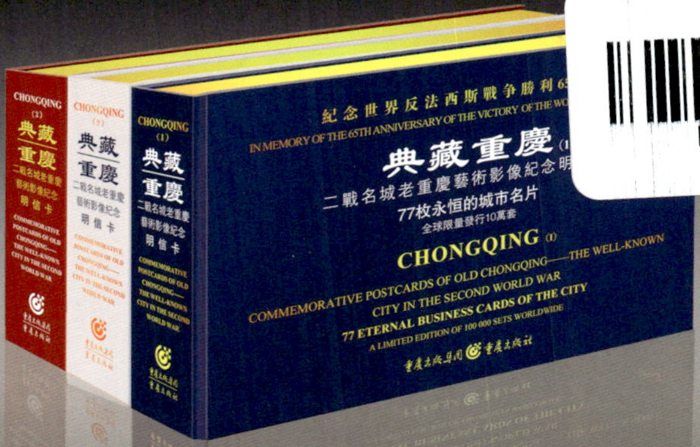

典藏重慶

二戰名城老重慶藝術影像紀念明信卡

每册77枚永恒的城市名片

全套（1-3册）

全球限量發行10萬套

《典藏重慶》（1）作品目録

1.拍攝理由(攝影者説） 2.晨霧中的重慶渝中區半島 3.朝天門 4.朝天門豐碑巷 5.千厮門 6.菜園壩 7.建興坡 8.東水門 9.太平門大碼頭 10.郵政局巷 南紀門 12.林森路 13.四方街 14-15.白象街吊脚樓民居 16.儲奇門大巷子 17.中興路小巷 18.馬蹄街 19.道門口商業金融區 20.洪崖洞 21.北區路 22.鹽銀行大樓 23.小什字 24.民族路 25.民權路 26.民生路正街 27.滄白路 28.五四路 29.國民政府外交部 30.較場口 31.倉壩子民居 32.金湯街 33.領巷 34.英國領事館 35.仁愛堂 36.四德村 37.黄家埡口 38.中一支路 39.枇杷山石階 40.國民政府立法院、司法院、蒙藏委員會及衛戍司令部舊址 41.兩口老街 42.美國大使館 43.羅斯福圖書館舊址 44.國民政府舊址 45.禮園 46.鵝嶺正街 47.嘉陵新村 48.牛角沱 49.高公館 50.劉湘舊居 51.化龍橋 十八集團軍(八路軍)重慶辦事處(紅岩村) 53.宋子文舊居 54.磁器口 55.美齡舞廳 56.蔣介石、毛澤東會談處 57.南岸老碼頭正街 58.海棠溪 59.長江南岸家灣民居 60.南岸周家灣相望渝中半島 61.玄壇廟 62.玄壇廟北望渝中半島 63.長江南岸黄家巷英國老宅 64.黄家巷民居 65.大法國水師兵營 66.黄桷古道君坡 67.德國大使館 68.抗戰時位于南山深處的蘇聯使館 69.總裁官邸 70-71.國民黨中央政治學校 72.範家花園 73.南温泉曾家公館 74.嘉陵江北岸渡口灘 75.嘉陵江北岸渡口石階 76.江北城保定門臨江民居 77.金剛碑 78.北碚草街子

《典藏重慶》（2）作品目録

1.建興坡 2.晨霧中的南區公園 3.白鶴亭 4.湖廣會館 5.湖廣會館正門 6.洪學巷 7.望龍門 8.望龍門石階 9.芝江巷老宅 10.黄荆巷 11.下伍家巷居 12.雷家坡 13.鳥瞰南紀門至山城巷 14.南紀門臨江民居 15.南紀門正街石階 16.川道拐 17.川道拐民居 18.宰房街 19.一字街 20.普安巷 21.興誠銀行 22.文化街 23.二府衙 24.打鑼巷 25.打鑼巷老宅 26.大來公司舊址 27.《新蜀報》舊址 28.重慶藥材同業公會舊址 29.刁家巷人家 30.凱路 31.抗戰時國民政府軍事委員會外事局 32.儲奇門大巷子 33.善果巷 34.月臺壩 35.鳳凰臺1號老宅 36.軍事委員會舊址 37.國民政府外交部 38.慈街 39.柑子堡 40.林森路西段（現解放西路） 41.林森路西段（現解放西路）民居 42.深巷人家 43.石板坡 44.白雲寺（石板坡新街35號） 45.石坡硝房溝右巷 46.千厮門正街 47.千厮門一號碼頭 48.洪崖洞 49.春至洪崖洞 50.紙鹽河巷 51.黄花園 52.黄花園居民 53.棉花街 54.保安路（現八路） 55.青年路 56.三民主義青年宫（現實驗劇場） 57.國民參政會舊址 58.小米市 59.民國路（現五一路） 60.民生路至臨江路口 61.十八梯吊脚樓市 62.十八梯吊脚樓 63.百子巷 64.唐式遵舊居 65.郭沫若舊居（天官府7號） 66.思園 67.韓國臨時政府舊址 68.保節院 69.通遠門街市 70.中山一小巷 71.中山一路119號老宅 72.歸元寺 73.中蘇文化協會舊址 74.蘇聯大使館 75.陳誠舊居 76.勝利路民居 77.抗戰勝利記功碑

《典藏重慶》（3）作品目録

1.黄家埡口 2.黄家埡口石階 3.黄家埡口民居 4.打槍壩水塔 5.蔣介石舊居和官邸 6.宋美齡舊居 7.德安裏李宗仁舊居 8.行政院舊址 9.康心遠舊居 10清寺 11.馬歇爾舊居 12.特園 13.遠東盟軍司令部及戰時兒童保育院 14.重慶市首任市長潘文華舊居 15.張治中舊居 16.沈鈞儒舊居 17.禮園石繩橋 18遠舉舊居 19.澳大利亞大使館 20.軍統第一電訊總臺 21.馮玉祥舊居 22.史迪威舊居 23.孫科舊居 24.白崇禧舊居 25.嘉陵江夕照 26.生生花園 27.李子正街 28.嘉陵新路76號老宅 29.國民政府軍事參議院（翰苑） 30.嘉陵新村老宅 31.國際研究所 32.土灣民居 33.津南村 34.國際廣播電臺 35.重慶大學學院 36.寅初亭 37.國民政府教育部 38.南開中學 39.國民政府三廳舊址 40.湯子敬（湯百萬）舊居 41.宋美齡舊居 42.蓮青樓 43.龍門浩老碼頭 44門浩老碼頭民居 45.南岸建業崗上眺看渝中半島 46.南岸建業崗140號 47.英國亞細亞火油公司舊址 48.英國立德樂洋行 49.英國海軍俱樂部 50.龍門浩米街 51.仁濟醫院 52.玄壇廟正街 53.彈子石 54.黄桷埡正街 55.陳布雷舊居 56.王陵基公館 57.杜月笙別墅 58.于右任舊居 59.空軍墳 60.軍委會侍從室所 61.陳立夫、陳果夫舊居 62-63.國民黨中央政治學校 64.孔祥熙舊居 65.日軍戰俘營 66.江北城渡口老宅 67.江北老城墻下的野渡 68.青草壩 69.黑子 70.黑石子河灘 71.北碚澄江鎮後街 72.最高法院 73.司法行政部 74.盧作孚舊居 75.老舍舊居 76.晏陽初舊居（晏宅） 77.北碚草街子（育才學校遺址

收藏一座城市的歷史，就是收藏這座城市的靈魂。

Collecting a city’s history is the collection of its soul.

典藏重慶·二戰名城老重慶藝術影像紀念明信卡（2）
DIANCANG CHONGQING

攝影編著　戴前鋒　翻譯　張兵一

出 版 人 羅小衛
策　　劃 劉　嘉　戴前鋒
責任編輯 劉　嘉
責任校對 胡　琳
設　　計 戴前鋒

重慶出版集團
重慶出版社 出版
重慶長江二路205號 郵政編碼：400016 http://www.cqph.com
重慶市金雅迪彩色印刷有限公司印製
重慶出版集團圖書發行有限公司發行
E-MAIL:fxchu@cqph.com 郵購電話：023-68809452
全國新華書店經銷

開本：889mm×1194mm 1/48 印張：3.25
2011年6月第1版 2012年6月第2次印刷
ISBN 978-7-229-03871-7

如有印裝質量問題，請向本集團圖書發行有限公司調換：023-68706683

拍攝理由 戴前鋒

鏡頭所到之處，没有哪座城市能像重慶這樣，其景觀形態與自身的多蹇命運統一得如此神形兼備。造物主爲中華大地預設的江域半島，在月涌大江孤帆、夕照雄關旌旗的曠古歲月中佇候，衹等待民族“存亡繼絶”的使命降臨。它像生命方舟，維係了國脈，蔭庇了積弱積貧的千萬生靈，最后悲劇性地凱旋於功成身退的歷史背影。無論史實如何演義，歷史的真相持久而頑强：重慶，一座江河環繞的山城半島，因處水陸要衝，遂成中國近代史上的“兩河流域”；又逢抗戰烽火，時稱中國最后的耶路撒冷；因其苦撑遠東戰局，譽同華盛頓、倫敦、莫斯科齊名的“二戰”名城。幽暗的民居、沉默的遺址所釋放出來的抗戰史實竟然毫不遜色於中外任何城市而成爲世界性話題。

Reasons for Photography Dai Qianfeng

I found the old city alive and beautiful with deeper aesthetic significance, and its natural appearance was so special that it seemed to imply its fateful hardships in history, which was rarely found elsewhere. This city built on the peninsula between two rivers looked just like an enormous ship, was it created to bear the heavy destiny of our country in the national crisis, like the Noah's Ark in the Christian world? The city was China's Mesopotamia in its modern history and the country's final Jerusalem in the Anti-Japanese War. It won for itself the great fame and tribute from the world just like Washington D.C., London and Moscow, recorded in those shadowed lanes and relics is its great resistance against Japanese invasion, as glory as any of the great ·ies in and out of China.

目録 Contents

建興坡
Jianxingpo

1

建興坡：位於菜園壩。這一帶是舊重慶典型的山城吊脚樓棚户區，現已全部拆除。

Jianxingpo: Situated in Caiyuanba, it used to be an area of typical wooden-pillar-supported houses and shabby huts, which were removed years ago.

貼郵
stamp

《典藏重慶》系列攝影作品（2） 重慶出版集团 重慶出版社
攝影編著：戴前鋒 翻譯：張兵一
SERIES PHOTO WORKS OF CHONGQING
PHOTOGRAPHER & COMPILER: DAI QIANFENG TRANSLATOR: ZHANG BINGYI

邮政编码 postcode

晨霧中的南區公園

Nanqu Park in the morning fog

2

晨霧中的南區公園

Nanqu Park in the morning fog

南區公園：位于菜園壩、建興坡一帶。

Nanqu Park was located around Caiyuanba and Jianxingpo.

貼郵

stamp

《典藏重慶》系列攝影作品（2） 重慶出版集团 重慶出版社

攝影編著：戴前鋒　翻譯：張兵一

SERIES PHOTO WORKS OF CHONGQING

PHOTOGRAPHER & COMPILER: DAI QIANFENG TRANSLATOR: ZHANG BINGYI

邮政编码 postcode

白鶴亭
Baihe (white crane) Pavilion

3

白鶴亭：舊時也稱陋巷，是朝天門與東水門城墻外的一條小巷。據故老講，此巷臨江一側有一橋一亭，橋上亭裏可望江對岸，塗山上時有許多白鶴從群山飛過，故名。

Baihe (white crane) Pavilion: Once also called the Shabby Lane, it was a small lane outside of the city wall between Chaotian Gate and Dongshui Gate. It is said that there used to be a bridge and a pavilion along its side by the river, from which white cranes could be seen flying over the Tushan Mountain on the other side of the Yangtze River.

貼郵
stamp

《典藏重慶》系列攝影作品 (2) 重慶出版集团 重慶出版社
攝影編著：戴前鋒　翻譯：張兵一
SERIES PHOTO WORKS OF CHONGQING
PHOTOGRAPHER & COMPILER: DAI QIANFENG TRANSLATOR: ZHANG BINGYI

邮政编码 postcode

貼郵
stamp

湖廣會館：明末清初四川遭受長期戰亂，人口鋭減，清定天下，開始向四川大規模移民。重慶是各地從水路來川移民主要落脚的地方，即時有湖廣、江西、福建、廣東、山西、陝西、浙江等會館成立。各省移民中湖廣最多，故有“湖廣填四川”之説。湖廣會館在下洪學巷，斜坡北側爲禹王宫。

Huguang Guild Hall: Sichuan suffered great decrease in population during the period of the late Ming Dynasty and early Qing Dynasty. The Qing government started large-scale immigration to the province after it conquered the whole China. Chongqing was the major destination for those immigrants coming by river route, many guild halls were built for those from Hunan, Hubei, Jiangxi, Fujian, Guangdong, Shanxi, Zhejiang, etc. The saying of “Huguang people filled Sichuan” showed the majority immigrants were from Hubei, Hunan and Guangdong. Huguang Guild Hall is located on Lower Hongxue Lane, to its north on the hillside is Yuwang Palace.

《典藏重慶》系列攝影作品 (2) 重慶出版集团 重慶出版社
攝影編著：戴前鋒　翻譯：張兵一
SERIES PHOTO WORKS OF CHONGQING
PHOTOGRAPHER & COMPILER: DAI QIANFENG TRANSLATOR: ZHANG BINGYI

邮政编码 postcode

湖廣會館正門
The gate of Huguang Guild Hall

5

贴邮
stamp

湖廣會館正門

The gate of Huguang Guild Hall

湖廣會館：明末清初四川遭受長期戰亂，人口鋭减，清定天下，開始向四川大規模移民。重慶是各地從水路來川移民主要落脚的地方，即時有湖廣、江西、福建、廣東、山西、陕西、浙江等會館成立。各省移民中湖廣最多，故有“湖廣填四川”之説。湖廣會館在下洪學巷，斜坡北側爲禹王宫。

Huguang Guild Hall: Sichuan suffered great decrease in population during the period of the late Ming Dynasty and early Qing Dynasty. The Qing government started large-scale immigration to the province after it conquered the whole China. Chongqing was the major destination for those immigrants coming by river route, many guild halls were built for those from Hunan, Hubei, Jiangxi, Fujian, Guangdong, Shanxi, Zhejiang, etc. The saying of “Huguang people filled Sichuan” showed the majority immigrants were from Hubei, Hunan and Guangdong. Huguang Guild Hall is located on Lower Hongxue Lane, to its north on the hillside is Yuwang Palace.

《典藏重慶》系列攝影作品 (2) 重慶出版集團 重慶出版社
攝影編著：戴前鋒　翻譯：張兵一
SERIES PHOTO WORKS OF CHONGQING
PHOTOGRAPHER & COMPILER: DAI QIANFENG TRANSLATOR: ZHANG BINGYI

邮政编码 postcode

洪學巷
Hongxue Lane

贴邮
stamp

洪學巷："洪"不是"黌"的簡筆字，但洪學巷的"洪"實際已與"黌"字同義。"黌"是學舍，黌學指巴縣文廟，建于南宋紹興年間。1928年巴縣第一高級小學遷此，抗日戰爭時期爲正陽學院。

Hongxue Lane: Hongxue means the Confucious temple in Baxian County, built in the Southern Song Dynasty (1127-1279). In 1928 the No. 1 Higher Primary School moved in the temple and was renamed Zheng Yang Institute during the Anti-Japanese War.

《典藏重慶》系列攝影作品 (2) 重慶出版集團 重慶出版社
攝影編著：戴前鋒 翻譯：張兵一
SERIES PHOTO WORKS OF CHONGQING
PHOTOGRAPHER & COMPILER: DAI QIANFENG TRANSLATOR: ZHANG BINGYI

邮政编码 postcode

望龍門
Wanglong Gate

贴邮
stamp

望龍門：位于渝中區南部偏東，在望龍門巷、望龍門碼頭與林森路（現解放東路）相交一帶，隔江與南岸龍門浩相峙，立此可望浩口巨石上南宋紹興時所鎸“龍門”二字，故名。望龍門系城區渡江通南岸的重要渡口，1944年7月至1945年4月，由茅以升、楊煬春主持設計、建造了重慶市第一條纜車道——望龍門纜車道，是爲中國内陸城市交通史上的創舉。

Wanglong Gate: Located east of the southern part of Yuzhong District, where Wanglong Gate Lane and Wanglong Gate Ferry meet with Lin Sen Road (now Jiefang Road), the place faced Longmenhao in Nan'an District across from the river. From the gate the inscription of Longmen (dragon gate) from the Southern Song Dynasty was clearly seen on the huge rock at Longmenhao. This is the important ferry to and from Nan'an District, and Chongqing's first cable car railway, designed by Mao Yisheng and Yang Yangchun, was built here as a great creation in the history of the country's inland communications.

《典藏重慶》系列攝影作品（2） 重慶出版集团 重慶出版社
攝影編著：戴前鋒　翻譯：張兵一
SERIES PHOTO WORKS OF CHONGQING
PHOTOGRAPHER & COMPILER: DAI QIANFENG TRANSLATOR: ZHANG BINGYI

邮政编码 postcode

望龍門石階

The steps at Wanglong Gate

貼郵
stamp

望龍門石階

The steps at Wanglong Gate

望龍門：位于渝中區南部偏東，在望龍門巷、望龍門碼頭與林森路（現解放東路）相交一帶，隔江與南岸龍門浩相峙，立此可望浩口巨石上南宋紹興時所鎸“龍門”二字，故名。望龍門系城區渡江通南岸的重要渡口，1944年7月至1945年4月，由茅以升、楊煬春主持設計、建造了重慶市第一條纜車道——望龍門纜車道，是爲中國内陸城市交通史上的創舉。

Wanglong Gate: Located east of the southern part of Yuzhong District, where Wanglong Gate Lane and Wanglong Gate Ferry meet with Lin Sen Road (now Jiefang Road), the place faced Longmenhao in Nan'an District across from the river. From the gate the inscription of Longmen (dragon gate) from the Southern Song Dynasty was clearly seen on the huge rock at Longmenhao. This is the important ferry to and from Nan'an District, and Chongqing's first cable car railway, designed by Mao Yisheng and Yang Yangchun, was built here as a great creation in the history of the country's inland communications.

《典藏重慶》系列攝影作品（2） 重慶出版集团 重慶出版社
攝影編著：戴前鋒　翻譯：張兵一
SERIES PHOTO WORKS OF CHONGQING
PHOTOGRAPHER & COMPILER: DAI QIANFENG　TRANSLATOR: ZHANG BINGYI

邮政编码 postcode

芝江巷老宅

The old houses at Zhijiang Lane

芝江巷老宅：巷名取義待考。民居依山而建，高低曲折（圖爲芝江巷10號老宅）。

The old houses at Zhijiang Lane: It is still unknown of the origin of the name. All old houses of Zhijiang Lane were built along the mountain slope. Shown in the picture are the ones in No.10, Zhijiang Lane.

貼郵
stamp

邮政编码 postcode

《典藏重慶》系列攝影作品 (2) 重慶出版集团 重慶出版社
攝影編著：戴前鋒 翻譯：張兵一
SERIES PHOTO WORKS OF CHONGQING
PHOTOGRAPHER & COMPILER: DAI QIANFENG TRANSLATOR: ZHANG BINGYI

貼郵
stamp

黄荆巷：原名黄荆街，在儲奇門外，城垣内爲儲奇門順城街，抗日戰爭時期蹇家巷、胡家巷并入。至今名稱未改。

Huangjing Lane: Used to be called Huangjing Street, it was located outside of Chuqi Gate, inside of which was Shuncheng Street. During the Anti-Japanese War Jianjia Lane and Hujia Lane were merged into the street.

《典藏重慶》系列攝影作品 (2) 重慶出版集團 重慶出版社
攝影編著：戴前鋒 翻譯：張兵一
SERIES PHOTO WORKS OF CHONGQING
PHOTOGRAPHER & COMPILER: DAI QIANFENG TRANSLATOR: ZHANG BINGYI

邮政编码 postcode

下伍家巷民居
The houses in Lower Wujia Lane

貼郵
stamp

下伍家巷民居：位于南紀門江邊。

The houses in Lower Wujia Lane: at Nanji Gate near the river.

《典藏重慶》系列攝影作品 (2) 重慶出版集团 重慶出版社
攝影編著：戴前鋒　翻譯：張兵一
SERIES PHOTO WORKS OF CHONGQING
PHOTOGRAPHER & COMPILER: DAI QIANFENG TRANSLATOR: ZHANG BINGYI

邮政编码 postcode

贴邮
stamp

雷家坡：位于南區路側陡坡上。民國初年，因雷姓人家居此得名，因地勢險峻，房屋大都建于石岩壁上，富有山城民居特色。

Leijiapo: It was located on the north hillside of Nanqu Road, named after the surname of the Lei families who used to live here at the beginning of the Republic of China. This residence was of typical Chongqing style for its houses built on the rocks on the mountain slope.

《典藏重慶》系列攝影作品（2） 重慶出版集团 重慶出版社
攝影編著：戴前鋒　翻譯：張兵一
SERIES PHOTO WORKS OF CHONGQING
PHOTOGRAPHER & COMPILER: DAI QIANFENG TRANSLATOR: ZHANG BINGYI

邮政编码 postcode

鳥瞰南紀門至山城巷

A bird's eye view of the area from Nanji Gate to Shancheng Lane

13

鳥瞰南紀門至山城巷

A bird's eye view of the area from Nanji Gate to Shancheng Lane

貼郵

stamp

《典藏重慶》系列攝影作品 (2) 重慶出版集団 重慶出版社

攝影編著：戴前鋒　翻譯：張兵一

SERIES PHOTO WORKS OF CHONGQING

PHOTOGRAPHER & COMPILER: DAI QIANFENG TRANSLATOR: ZHANG BINGYI

邮政编码 postcode

南紀門臨江民居
Residence by river in Nanji Gate

貼郵
stamp

南紀門臨江民居

Residence by river in Nanji Gate

南紀門：重慶十七門之一，位于長江之濱，舊時城門（現不存）上書“南屏擁翠”。此地爲木材集散地和屠宰業集中處。其得名，相傳源于《詩經・小雅・四月》：“滔滔江漢，南國之紀。”

Nanji Gate: Used to be one of the 17 old city gates, it stands by the Yangtze River, on which was written Southern Shield in Green. The Gate is long gone. This place was once the distributing center of lumber and slaughterhouses.

《典藏重慶》系列攝影作品 (2) 重慶出版集团 重慶出版社
攝影編著：戴前鋒　翻譯：張兵一
SERIES PHOTO WORKS OF CHONGQING
PHOTOGRAPHER & COMPILER: DAI QIANFENG TRANSLATOR: ZHANG BINGYI

邮政编码 postcode

南紀門正街石階
The flights of stone steps in Nanjimen Zhengjie

貼郵
stamp

南紀門正街石階

The flights of stone steps in Nanjimen Zhengjie

南紀門：重慶十七門之一，位于長江之濱，舊時城門（現不存）上書"南屏擁翠"。此地爲木材集散地和屠宰業集中處。其得名，相傳源于《詩經・小雅・四月》："滔滔江漢，南國之紀。"

Nanji Gate: Used to be one of the 17 old city gates, it stands by the Yangtze River, on which was written Southern Shield in Green. The Gate is long gone. This place was once the distributing center of lumber and slaughterhouses.

《典藏重慶》系列攝影作品 (2) 重慶出版集团 重慶出版社
攝影編著：戴前鋒　翻譯：張兵一
SERIES PHOTO WORKS OF CHONGQING
PHOTOGRAPHER & COMPILER: DAI QIANFENG TRANSLATOR: ZHANG BINGYI

邮政编码 postcode

貼郵
stamp

川道拐：是重慶的東大門，出川的必經之道。抗戰前，成渝客商、挑夫來往于此，成爲頗有名氣的一條商業通道，它與一字街、宰房街、二支巷形成商業街區。

Chuandaoguai: The eastern gate of Chongqing, Chuandaoguai used to be the start of the important road leading out of Sichuan. Before the Anti-Japanese War it had been a well-known street of commerce, as part of the city's commercial area together with Yizi Street, Zaifang Street and Erzhi Lane.

《典藏重慶》系列攝影作品 (2) 重慶出版集团 重慶出版社
攝影編著：戴前鋒　翻譯：張兵一
SERIES PHOTO WORKS OF CHONGQING
PHOTOGRAPHER & COMPILER: DAI QIANFENG TRANSLATOR: ZHANG BINGYI

邮政编码 postcode

川道拐民居

The residence at Chuandaoguai

贴邮

stamp

川道拐民居

The residence at Chuandaoguai

川道拐：是重慶的東大門，出川的必經之道。抗戰前，成渝客商、挑夫來往于此，成爲頗有名氣的一條商業通道，它與一字街、宰房街、二支巷形成商業街區。

Chuandaoguai: The eastern gate of Chongqing, Chuandaoguai used to be the start of the important road leading out of Sichuan. Before the Anti-Japanese War it had been a well-known street of commerce, as part of the city's commercial area together with Yizi Street, Zaifang Street and Erzhi Lane.

《典藏重慶》系列攝影作品（2） 重慶出版集团 重慶出版社
攝影編著：戴前鋒　翻譯：張兵一
SERIES PHOTO WORKS OF CHONGQING
PHOTOGRAPHER & COMPILER: DAI QIANFENG TRANSLATOR: ZHANG BINGYI

邮政编码 postcode

贴邮
stamp

宰房街：位于川道拐一带，牲畜屠宰地，據説宰牛餘下的下水廉價出售，有馬氏兄弟在此開了一家以牛毛肚爲主要菜品的紅湯火鍋，是當今重慶火鍋業的源頭。

Zaifang Street: The street used to be a place for livestock butchery and selling of internal organs. It was said that the first hot pot in Chongqing was started here by two brothers surnamed Ma, who served mostly hot hog bowels of oxen.

《典藏重慶》系列攝影作品（2） 重慶出版集团 重慶出版社
攝影編著：戴前鋒 翻譯：張兵一
SERIES PHOTO WORKS OF CHONGQING
PHOTOGRAPHER & COMPILER: DAI QIANFENG TRANSLATOR: ZHANG BINGYI

邮政编码 postcode

貼郵
stamp

一字街：位于川道拐一帶。

Yizi Street was located near Chuandaoguai

川道拐：是重慶的東大門，出川的必經之道。抗戰前，成渝客商、挑夫來往于此，成爲頗有名氣的一條商業通道，它與一字街、宰房街、二支巷形成商業街區。

Chuandaoguai: The eastern gate of Chongqing, Chuandaoguai used to be the start of the important road leading out of Sichuan. Before the Anti-Japanese War it had been a well-known street of commerce, as part of the city's commercial area together with Yizi Street, Zaifang Street and Erzhi Lane.

《典藏重慶》系列攝影作品（2） 重慶出版集团 重慶出版社
攝影編著：戴前鋒　翻譯：張兵一
SERIES PHOTO WORKS OF CHONGQING
PHOTOGRAPHER & COMPILER: DAI QIANFENG TRANSLATOR: ZHANG BINGYI

邮政编码 postcode

普安巷
Pu'an Lane

贴邮
stamp

普安巷：因此地有普安堂得名。100年前，重慶第一臺直流發電機從這裏發電。1906年（清光緒三十二年）11月28日，時任重慶商務總會總理的李耀庭70壽辰，巴縣商紳劉沛膏在普安堂安裝的100千瓦直流發電機首次供電李府，50盞燈齊明，從此重慶有了電力資源。

Pu'an Lane: This name came from the Pu'an Church in the lane. 100 years ago the first direct-current generator in the city started working for the 50 electric lamps in Li's Mansion on accassion of the 70th birthday of Li Yaoting, Chairman of Chongqing General Chamber of Commerce. The 100-kilowatt generator was sent to him as a gift by Liu Peigao, a rich businessman from Baxian County.

《典藏重慶》系列攝影作品 (2) 重慶出版集团 重慶出版社
攝影编著：戴前鋒 翻譯：張兵一
SERIES PHOTO WORKS OF CHONGQING
PHOTOGRAPHER & COMPILER: DAI QIANFENG TRANSLATOR: ZHANG BINGYI

邮政编码 postcode

貼郵

stamp

聚興誠銀行：位于林森路東，這是著名的聚興誠銀行的舊址。銀行是由楊氏家族獨資經營的聚興誠商號的一部分資金轉化而來，銀行的英文招牌叫楊氏弟兄公司。楊氏家族創業人楊文光（名焕門），派子侄去日本、美國深造。次子楊希仲（名培賢）十分羡慕三井、三菱等大壟斷財閥，不斷向父親建議組建銀行。1913年回國后創建聚興誠銀行，由留日工程師黎治平仿日本三井銀行設計新建大厦，聚興誠銀行于1915年4月1日開業。

Juxingcheng Bank: The former site of the famous Juxingcheng Bank on the east side of Lin Sen Road. The bank was set up with part of the capital of Yang Brothers Company, owned by the Yang family. Yang Wenguang, the founder of the company, sent his son and niece to study in Japan and the United States in determination of increasing his business. Yang Xizhong was his second son who repeatedly suggested to him for establishment of bank business. In 1913 the son returned home, and founded the bank. The building was designed by Li Zhiping, an engineer who studied in Japan, in imitation of Japanese Mitsui bank. Juxingcheng Bank was open on April 1st, 1915.

《典藏重慶》系列攝影作品 (2) 重慶出版集团 重慶出版社
攝影編著：戴前鋒　翻譯：張兵一
SERIES PHOTO WORKS OF CHONGQING
PHOTOGRAPHER & COMPILER: DAI QIANFENG TRANSLATOR: ZHANG BINGYI

邮政编码 postcode

贴邮
stamp

文化街：是上半城與下半城間主要通道之一，以文昌宫得名。文昌宫建于唐開元二年（公元714年）。

Wenhua Street: One of the main streets connecting the upper and lower cities, the street was named after Wenchang Palace built in 714, the Tang Dynasty.

《典藏重慶》系列攝影作品（2）重慶出版集團 重慶出版社
攝影編著：戴前鋒　翻譯：張兵一
SERIES PHOTO WORKS OF CHONGQING
PHOTOGRAPHER & COMPILER: DAI QIANFENG TRANSLATOR: ZHANG BINGYI

邮政编码 postcode

中西医

貼郵
stamp

二府衙：原名二府衙街。此街本來也是上半城與下半城之間的通道，少爲人注意。原巴縣城隍廟舊址就在二府衙巷口的北側。二府衙是同知署的俗稱（同知系知府佐貳，習稱二府），原在此街。二府衙19號是1925—1927年中共四川省委地方委員會舊址，也是楊闇公的舊居。

Erfuya: Originally Erfuya Street, it used to be one of the connections between the upper and lower cities. On the northern side of the beginning of the lane there used to be a town god's temple of Baxian County. Erfuya was the vulgar name for "yamen"---the government office in feudal China. No.19, Erfuya was the former location of CPC Sichuan Committee during 1925-1927, and the residence of Yang Angong, the first secretary of the committee.

《典藏重慶》系列攝影作品 (2) 重慶出版集團 重慶出版社
攝影編著：戴前鋒 翻譯：張兵一
SERIES PHOTO WORKS OF CHONGQING
PHOTOGRAPHER & COMPILER: DAI QIANFENG TRANSLATOR: ZHANG BINGYI

邮政编码 postcode

打鑼巷：舊時鳴鑼報時得名。

Daluo Lane: It was named after the gong beating for time in history.

貼郵
stamp

《典藏重慶》系列攝影作品(2) 重慶出版集團 重慶出版社
攝影編著：戴前鋒 翻譯：張兵一
SERIES PHOTO WORKS OF CHONGQING
PHOTOGRAPHER & COMPILER: DAI QIANFENG TRANSLATOR: ZHANG BINGYI

邮政编码 postcode

打鑼巷老宅
The old houses in Daluo Lane

貼郵
stamp

打鑼巷老宅：舊時鳴鑼報時得名。

The old houses in Daluo Lane

《典藏重慶》系列攝影作品（2） 重慶出版集团 重慶出版社
攝影編著：戴前鋒　翻譯：張兵一
SERIES PHOTO WORKS OF CHONGQING
PHOTOGRAPHER & COMPILER: DAI QIANFENG TRANSLATOR: ZHANG BINGYI

邮政编码 postcode

大來公司舊址
The former site of Dalai Company

贴邮
stamp

大來公司舊址：位于渝中區白象街142號，始建于1850年。整體建築風格呈現歐洲文藝復興時期風格，是白象街最具有特色的老建築。歷史上，這裏也曾是汪全泰號絲綢商鋪。

The former site of Dalai Company: Located at No.142, Baixiang Street, Yuzhong District, and built in 1850, it was the the most typical old building in the street, with the style of European renaissance. It also used to be the shop of Wang Quantai Silks Company.

邮政编码 postcode

《典藏重慶》系列攝影作品（2） 重慶出版集团 重慶出版社
攝影编著：戴前鋒 翻譯：張兵一
SERIES PHOTO WORKS OF CHONGQING
PHOTOGRAPHER & COMPILER: DAI QIANFENG TRANSLATOR: ZHANG BINGYI

《新蜀報》舊址

The former location of *New Sichuan Newspaper*

貼郵
stamp

《新蜀報》舊址：位于白象街115號，是一座雙朝門院落，第二道朝門横額行書“秀挹羊城”四個大字。此報由少年中國學會會員陳愚生和銅元局局長鮮英創辦，1921年2月1日正式出版，由周欽岳先生主持。

The former location of *New Sichuan Newspaper*: This is a double-gate garden located at No.115, Baixiang Street. The paper was founded by Chen Yusheng, member of China Juvenile Institution and Xian Ying, head of the National Standard Currency Mint, first published on Feburary 1st, 1921, with Mr. Zhou Qinyue as its editor in chief.

《典藏重慶》系列攝影作品 (2) 重庆出版集团 重庆出版社
攝影編著：戴前鋒　翻譯：張兵一
SERIES PHOTO WORKS OF CHONGQING
PHOTOGRAPHER & COMPILER: DAI QIANFENG TRANSLATOR: ZHANG BINGYI

邮政编码 postcode

重慶藥材同業公會舊址

The former site of Chongqing Medicinal Materials Trade Association

貼郵
stamp

重慶藥材同業公會舊址：位于儲奇門羊子壩15號，瀕臨長江，建于1926年6月。公會大樓具有巴洛克風格，呈折衷主義特色，但紋樣細節又表現出中國民間雜寶吉祥和瓜果藥材圖案，是重慶早期建築中不多見的中西合璧建築。著名實業家、重慶商會主席温少鶴曾在樓内創辦了山城中學（今五十三中學）。

The former site of Chongqing Medicinal Materials Trade Association: Located at No.15, Yangziba, Chuqi Gate, the house was built in June, 1926, as a baroque building with Chinese auspicious mortifs, melons and fruits. It was a rare combination of both Chinese and western architectural styles among the city's early architectures. It was in this building Wen Shaohe, a well-kown industrialist and chairman of Chongqing Chamber of Commerce, established Shancheng Middle School---the present No.53 Middle School.

《典藏重慶》系列攝影作品 (2) 重慶出版集团 重慶出版社
攝影編著：戴前鋒　翻譯：張兵一
SERIES PHOTO WORKS OF CHONGQING
PHOTOGRAPHER & COMPILER: DAI QIANFENG TRANSLATOR: ZHANG BINGYI

邮政编码 postcode

刁家巷人家：刁家巷是重慶上下半城間主要通道之一。

The residence in Diaojia Lane: One of the main connections between the upper and lower cities.

貼郵
stamp

《典藏重慶》系列攝影作品 (2) 重慶出版集团 重慶出版社
攝影编著：戴前鋒　翻譯：張兵一
SERIES PHOTO WORKS OF CHONGQING
PHOTOGRAPHER & COMPILER: DAI QIANFENG TRANSLATOR: ZHANG BINGYI

邮政编码 postcode

貼郵
stamp

凱旋路：位于渝中區東南部，北起較場口交中正路（現新華路）、磁器街，南止儲奇門接林森路（現解放路）。凱旋路的修建，是溝通上下半城幹道的巨大工程，從1940年開工到1942年4月才完成。主要工程由石堡坎和石拱旱橋組成，取"抗戰勝利凱旋歸來"之意命名。抗戰時國民政府軍事委員會外事局、軍政部、軍令部第一、二廳等軍事機構位于此路（現凱旋路中學一帶）。

Kaixuan Road: Located in the southeastern part of Yuzhong District, the road started from Zhongzheng Road (now Xinhua Road) and Ciqi Street of Jiaochangkou at north and ended at Lin Sen Road and Chuqi Gate at south. As the main connection between the upper and lower parts of the city, Kaixuan Road was built from 1940 to April, 1942, many parts of it were supported by stone slope walls and stone arch viaducts. "Kaixuan" meant the "victory of the Anti-Japanese War". Along the road near the present Kaixuan Road Middle School, there used to be many KMT government units, such as the Bureau of Foreign Affairs of Military Committee, Military and Administrative Ministry, the first and second departments of Military Orders Ministry.

《典藏重慶》系列攝影作品 (2) 重慶出版集團 重慶出版社
攝影編著：戴前鋒　翻譯：張兵一
SERIES PHOTO WORKS OF CHONGQING
PHOTOGRAPHER & COMPILER: DAI QIANFENG TRANSLATOR: ZHANG BINGYI

邮政编码 postcode

抗戰時國民政府軍事委員會外事局

The Foreign Affairs Bureau of Military Committee of the nationalist government during the Anti-Japanese War

抗戰時國民政府軍事委員會外事局：位于今凱旋路中學内。

The Foreign Affairs Bureau of Military Committee of the nationalist government during the Anti-Japanese War: located in the present Kaixuan Road Middle School.

貼郵
stamp

《典藏重慶》系列攝影作品 (2) 重慶出版集团 重慶出版社
攝影編著：戴前鋒　翻譯：張兵一
SERIES PHOTO WORKS OF CHONGQING
PHOTOGRAPHER & COMPILER: DAI QIANFENG TRANSLATOR: ZHANG BINGYI

邮政编码 postcode

貼郵
stamp

儲奇門大巷子：儲奇門位于渝中區東南部，爲重慶十七座城門中九開門之一，明洪武初砌石築城，月城城門面向長江上游。舊時爲山貨、藥材集散地，多山貨藥商字號、堆棧，民間俗諺稱“藥材行，百病治”。命名“儲奇”，含有預兆城豐、祈願昌盛之意。1927年後城市建設中城垣拆除。儲奇門大巷子原名“大巷子”，已歷多年，在“文革”中變成“儲奇門大巷子”，此巷也是溝通上下半城的通道，但不爲人所注意。

Chuqi Gate Daxiangzi: The gate was situated in the southeastern part of Yuzhong District, one of the 9 open gates among the 17 ones. The stone wall was built in the Ming Dynasty, with a satellite town facing the upper reaches of the Yangtze River. The place used to be a distribution center of mountain products and herbal medicine. “Chuqi” meant “prosperity” of the city. The wall was dismantled in 1927 for city expansion. Originally the lane had been called Daxiangzi, renamed as it was during the Great Cultural Revolution. It was also one of the connections between the upper and lower parts of the city, but few people ever noticed.

《典藏重慶》系列攝影作品 (2) 重慶出版集团 重慶出版社
攝影編著：戴前鋒　翻譯：張兵一
SERIES PHOTO WORKS OF CHONGQING
PHOTOGRAPHER & COMPILER: DAI QIANFENG TRANSLATOR: ZHANG BINGYI

邮政编码 postcode

貼郵
stamp

善果巷：位于較場口南沿坎下。清末，居民爲便夜間行人，自發湊錢買油點燈，取善果有報得名。此處曾有觀音岩廟一座。1940年被日機炸毀後，在原廟地修建棚戶安置被炸居民，廟主後又重新修建此廟，“文革”中被毀。

Shanguo Lane: Located below the southern ridge of Jiaochangkou, the lane was named for the philanthropic act of local people who raised money to light the lane during the late Qing Dynasty. There used to be a Guanyingyan Temple, which was destroyed by Japanese bombardment in 1940, and temporary shelters were built on the site for the homeless residents after the bombardment. The temple was rebult by the head priest and dismantled during the Cultural Revolution.

《典藏重慶》系列攝影作品 (2) 重慶出版集团 重慶出版社
攝影編著：戴前鋒　翻譯：張兵一
SERIES PHOTO WORKS OF CHONGQING
PHOTOGRAPHER & COMPILER: DAI QIANFENG TRANSLATOR: ZHANG BINGYI

邮政编码 postcode

贴邮
stamp

月臺壩：位于較場口南沿坎下。1916年胡子昂之父胡于成在此建公館，門前修有半圓形地壩，酷似彎月故名。

Yuetaiba: Located below the southern ridge of Jiaochangkou, it was the place where Hu Yucheng, Hu Zi'ang's father, built his residence in 1916. The place was so called because of the courtyard in front of the residence, which looked like a half-moon.

《典藏重慶》系列攝影作品（2） 重慶出版集團 重慶出版社
攝影編著：戴前鋒 翻譯：張兵一
SERIES PHOTO WORKS OF CHONGQING
PHOTOGRAPHER & COMPILER: DAI QIANFENG TRANSLATOR: ZHANG BINGYI

邮政编码 postcode

鳳凰臺1號老宅

The old houses at No.1, Fenghuangtai

貼郵
stamp

鳳凰臺1號老宅：向楚《巴縣·古迹》中說：“在南紀門內右營署前，昔傳有鳳凰鳴其上”，後有鳳凰池，故名。鳳凰臺1號老宅是一處有重要景觀意義的臨街建築群。建于清末民初，中西合璧風格，坐北朝南。陪都時期，政府社會部、軍政部運輸處、軍政部軍糧食總局、重慶地方法院審判廳，法國大使館等落址于此。

The old houses at No.1, Fenghuangtai: According to historical records, Fenghuangtai(Phoenix Platform) was located inside of Nanji Gate, so named because of the legend that a phoenix had been seen chirping on the platform. No.1 houses along the road were of historic interest, which were built during the late Qing Dynasty and early period of the Republic of China, with both Chinese and western styles. During the Anti-Japanese War, the place was the location of the Social Ministry, the Communications Department and General Bureau of Army Provisions of KMT's Military and Administrative Ministry, the tribunal of Chongqing District Court and the French Embassy.

《典藏重慶》系列攝影作品 (2) 重慶出版集团 重慶出版社
攝影編著：戴前鋒　翻譯：張兵一
SERIES PHOTO WORKS OF CHONGQING
PHOTOGRAPHER & COMPILER: DAI QIANFENG TRANSLATOR: ZHANG BINGYI

邮政编码 postcode

軍事委員會舊址

The former site of Military Committee of the nationalist government

貼郵
stamp

軍事委員會舊址：此處清代爲重慶鎮署，辛亥革命後改爲重慶鎮撫府。抗日戰爭爆發後，國民政府移駐重慶，1939年2月軍事委員會遷此辦公。抗戰勝利后，1945年9月4日蔣介石在此舉行了慶祝抗戰勝利茶會，9月18日國民參政會在此舉行茶會紀念“九一八”，10月8日軍事委員會政治部主任張治中在此舉行了盛大宴會，毛澤東、周恩來都應邀參加。

This used to be the government office of Chongqing in the Qing Dynasty and after the 1911 Revolution. The Military Committee moved here in Feburary, 1939 when the nationalist government moved to Chongqing after the breakout of the Anti-Japanese War. After the victory of the war, Chiang Kai-shek held a tea party here for celebration on September 4th, 1945, and on 18th the same month another tea party was held here by the Consultation Committee in memory of the “9•18 Incident”, an incident took place on September 18, 1931 which resulted in Japanese militarists' massive invasion in Northeastern China and later in the whole country in 1937. And on 8th, October Mr. Zhang Zhizhong, head of Political Department of Military Committee, held a large-scale banquet for the victory, attended by Mao Zedong, Zhou Enlai, among others.

《典藏重慶》系列攝影作品 (2) 重庆出版集团 重庆出版社
攝影編著：戴前鋒　翻譯：張兵一
SERIES PHOTO WORKS OF CHONGQING
PHOTOGRAPHER & COMPILER: DAI QIANFENG　TRANSLATOR: ZHANG BINGYI

邮政编码 postcode

國民政府外交部
Ministry of Foreign Affairs

國民政府外交部：位于林森路（現解放西路）112號。外交部爲行政院下屬部門，設總務、東亞、西亞、美洲、條約、情報等司。從1941年到1945年，外交部長爲宋子文，抗戰時期該部工作成績顯赫，時稱“陪都外交”。

Ministry of Foreign Affairs of the nationalist government was situated at No.112, Lin Sen Road (the present West Jiefang Road). The Ministry was under the Executive Yuan, including departments such as General Administration, East Asia, West Asia, America, Conventions and Intelligence, with Song Ziwen as the minister from 1941 to 1945. The foreign affairs during the Anti-Japanese War were usually called "Peidu Diplomacy" (Wartime Capital Diplomacy) for its obvious successful work.

《典藏重慶》系列攝影作品 (2) 重慶出版集团 重慶出版社
攝影编著：戴前鋒 翻譯：張兵一
SERIES PHOTO WORKS OF CHONGQING
PHOTOGRAPHER & COMPILER: DAI QIANFENG TRANSLATOR: ZHANG BINGYI

貼郵
stamp

邮政编码 postcode

貼郵
stamp

厚慈街：此地舊時夜間小吃攤遍布，亮油燈壺燃亮街巷，得“好吃街”名。當局嫌此名不雅，以街内有一用于防火的浩大水池更名“浩池街”，后合并其他小巷，命名“厚慈街”。1930年5月5日，中共地下黨四川省委書記劉願庵及主要成員在厚慈街裕發祥醬園鋪秘密據點開會時被當局逮捕。

Houci Street: The street used to be a night market for snacks, with vendors' stands lighted by oil-lamps along its length, therefore it was originally called Haochi Street, literally meaning "like to eat". It was changed into another "haochi", meaning "large pond", after the large pond in the street because the local authorities thought the original was vulgar. It was finally named as Houci Street after it was merged with other small lanes nearby. On May 5th, 1930 Liu Yuan'an, the underground CPC secretary of Sichuan Province and his comrades were arrested here when they were having a secret meeting in Yufaxiang Sauce & Pickles Shop.

《典藏重慶》系列攝影作品（2） 重慶出版集团 重慶出版社
攝影編著：戴前鋒　翻譯：張兵一
SERIES PHOTO WORKS OF CHONGQING
PHOTOGRAPHER & COMPILER: DAI QIANFENG　TRANSLATOR: ZHANG BINGYI

邮政编码 postcode

貼郵
stamp

柑子堡：位于中興路側，清末，因此處多種柑子樹得名。抗戰時期，國民政府賑濟委員會和中央救灾準備金保管委員會曾設于柑子堡15號。

Ganzibao: Located at Zhongxing Road, the place was named after the orange trees growing here during the late Qing Dynasty. During the Anti-Japanese War, the Disaster Relief Committee of the nationalist government and Disaster Relief Fund Committee of the KMT Central Committee were stationed here.

《典藏重慶》系列攝影作品（2） 重慶出版集团 重慶出版社
攝影編著：戴前鋒 翻譯：張兵一
SERIES PHOTO WORKS OF CHONGQING
PHOTOGRAPHER & COMPILER: DAI QIANFENG TRANSLATOR: ZHANG BINGYI

邮政编码 postcode

林森路西段（現解放西路）

The western part of Lin Sen Road (the present West Jiefang Road)

貼郵
stamp

林森路西段（現解放西路）

The western part of Lin Sen Road (the present West Jiefang Road)

林森路（現解放東路至解放西路）：過去的重慶城繁盛區域在下半城，下半城的主幹街道在朝天門一帶。抗日戰爭時期國民政府遷駐重慶，對此處拓寬改建，調整部分街道名稱，以當時國民政府主席林森之名命此路爲“林森路”。

Lin Sen Road (from the present East Jiefang Road to West Jiefang Road): The "lower part" of Chongqing used to be the most prosperous place of the city, whereas the busiest streets were around Chaotian Gate. Parts of the old streets in the place were broadened and renamed after the nationalist government moved to Chongqing during the Anti-Japanese War. Lin Sen Road was named after the then Chairman of the nationalist government.

《典藏重慶》系列攝影作品（2） 重慶出版集团 重慶出版社
攝影編著：戴前鋒　翻譯：張兵一
SERIES PHOTO WORKS OF CHONGQING
PHOTOGRAPHER & COMPILER: DAI QIANFENG TRANSLATOR: ZHANG BINGYI

邮政编码 postcode

林森路西段（現解放西路）民居

The residence of the western part of Lin Sen Road(the present West Jiefang Road)

貼郵
stamp

林森路西段（現解放西路）民居

The residence of the western part of Lin Sen Road (the present West Jiefang Road)

林森路（現解放東路至解放西路）：過去的重慶城繁盛的區域在下半城，下半城的主幹街道在朝天門一帶。抗日戰争時期國民政府遷駐重慶，對此處拓寬改建，調整部分街道名稱，以當時國民政府主席林森之名命此路爲“林森路”。

Lin Sen Road (from the present East Jiefang Road to West Jiefang Road): The “lower part” of Chongqing used to be the most prosperous place of the city, whereas the busiest streets were around Chaotian Gate. Parts of the old streets in the place were broadened and renamed after the nationalist government moved to Chongqing during the Anti-Japanese War. Lin Sen Road was named after the then Chairman of the nationalist government.

《典藏重慶》系列攝影作品 (2) 重慶出版集團 重慶出版社
攝影編著：戴前鋒　翻譯：張兵一
SERIES PHOTO WORKS OF CHONGQING
PHOTOGRAPHER & COMPILER: DAI QIANFENG TRANSLATOR: ZHANG BINGYI

邮政编码 postcode

贴邮
stamp

深巷人家

The residence in a deep lane

《典藏重慶》系列攝影作品 (2) 重慶出版集团 重慶出版社

攝影編著：戴前鋒　翻譯：張兵一

SERIES PHOTO WORKS OF CHONGQING

PHOTOGRAPHER & COMPILER: DAI QIANFENG TRANSLATOR: ZHANG BINGYI

邮政编码 postcode

贴邮
stamp

石板坡：位于城内南部，是半島山脊通遠門外南坡上的一片街巷，呈梯形。過去的石板坡是荒山坡中孤零零的一條路，行人稀少，因有一處采石場，故名。重慶建市后，1933年南區公路修通，人口增多形成街巷。

Shibanpo: This area included several streets and lanes on the south hillside outside of Tongyuan Gate. It used to be a large piece of barren land with a single lane through it, its name was chosen for the stone pit in the place. When Chongqing won its status of a city, more streets and lanes were built after the appearance of Nanqu Road in 1933.

《典藏重慶》系列攝影作品（2） 重庆出版集团 重庆出版社
攝影編著：戴前鋒　翻譯：張兵一
SERIES PHOTO WORKS OF CHONGQING
PHOTOGRAPHER & COMPILER: DAI QIANFENG TRANSLATOR: ZHANG BINGYI

邮政编码 postcode

白雲寺（石板坡新街35號）
Baiyun Temple (No. 35, Shibanpo Xinjie)

贴邮
stamp

白雲寺（石板坡新街35號）：白雲寺原名白雲觀，在石板坡新村東側門，門牌33號。1949年后，住持被列爲“一貫道”加以追究。而住持的辦法多，把道觀變爲和尚廟，并得到佛教協會的承認，白雲觀便成了白雲寺，才告無事。自然，以后白雲寺仍然没有受到宗教組織對待，變成了民居。

Baiyun Temple (No. 35, Shibanpo Xinjie): Baiyun Temple was originally called Baiyun Taoist Temple, located at No.33, east of Shibanpo New Village. It was changed into a Buddist temple after 1949. In the later years it was gradually changed into a residence house, but the name remained.

《典藏重慶》系列攝影作品（2） 重慶出版集团 重慶出版社
攝影編著：戴前鋒　翻譯：張兵一
SERIES PHOTO WORKS OF CHONGQING
PHOTOGRAPHER & COMPILER: DAI QIANFENG TRANSLATOR: ZHANG BINGYI

邮政编码 postcode

石板坡硝房沟右巷
Xiaofanggou You Lane, Shibanpo

貼郵
stamp

石板坡硝房溝右巷：原名硝房溝右街，位于石板坡地區西沿。硝房溝是以行業命名，硝房是皮革工廠，即以樸硝鞣皮革的工廠。其實這裏并不是硝房集中的地區，硝房溝右巷西側衹有幾間硝房加工生牛皮（也有羊皮），下石板坡地區的川道拐才是集中宰牛的地方。硝房集中在與川道拐相接的一字街，硝房溝衹有幾家硝房，是一字街容納不下延伸而來的。

Xiaofanggou You Lane, Shibanpo: This was a lane along the west side of Shibanpo area, used to be called Xiaofanggou You Street. “Xiaofang” meant tanyards, though this was not the largest place for the industry. There were only a few tanyards for rawhide of cows and sheeps, and Yizi Street was the real place for leather processing, connecting with which was Chuandaoguai of the Lower Shibanpo, the slaughterhouse of cows.

《典藏重慶》系列攝影作品（2） 重慶出版集团 重慶出版社
攝影編著：戴前鋒　翻譯：張兵一
SERIES PHOTO WORKS OF CHONGQING
PHOTOGRAPHER & COMPILER: DAI QIANFENG TRANSLATOR: ZHANG BINGYI

邮政编码 postcode

千厮門正街
Qiansi Gate Zhengjie Street

貼郵
stamp

千廝門正街：清末的千廝門正街是現在的千廝門行街，現在的千廝門正街，是過去出入千廝門瓮城門與紙鹽河街（巷）之間的那一小段石梯路。出城下坡，進城上坡，城門不在而石梯猶存。

千廝門：宋末即有記載的古城門（城門現不存）。位於長江、嘉陵江匯合江岸。江岸爲嘉陵江水系來往貨船停泊處，是中藥、紙、鹽、煤的集散地。其得名，相傳源於《詩·小雅·甫田》："曾孫之稼，如茨如梁；曾孫之庾，如坻如京。乃求千廝倉，乃求萬廝箱……"寓意五谷豐登，糧食滿倉，一派豐收年景。

Qiansi Gate Zhengjie Street: In the late Qing Dynasty, the street was called the New Qiansi Gate Street, a short passway of stone steps between the satellite town of Qiansi Gate and Zhiyanhe Street. Now the stone steps remain though the city gate is no more existent.

Qiansi Gate: No more existent, the Gate was at the joint point of the Yangtze and Jialing rivers, first recorded in writing as early as the Song Dynasty(960~1279). This used to be the berth area for the boats on the Jialing River, as well as the distributing center of traditional Chinese medicine, paper, salt and coal. The name Qiansi came from a famous ancient Chinese poem which means good harvest and prosperity.

《典藏重慶》系列攝影作品（2） 重慶出版集团 重慶出版社
攝影編著：戴前鋒 翻譯：張兵一
SERIES PHOTO WORKS OF CHONGQING
PHOTOGRAPHER & COMPILER: DAI QIANFENG TRANSLATOR: ZHANG BINGYI

邮政编码 postcode

千厮门一號碼頭

No.1 Wharf, Qiansi Gate

貼郵
stamp

千厮門一號碼頭

No.1 Wharf, Qiansi Gate

千厮門：宋末即有記載的古城門（城門現不存）。位於長江、嘉陵江匯合江岸。江岸爲嘉陵江水系來往貨船停泊處，是中藥、紙、鹽、煤的集散地。其得名，相傳源於《詩・小雅・甫田》："曾孫之稼，如茨如梁；曾孫之庾，如坻如京。乃求千厮倉，乃求萬厮箱……"寓意五谷豐登，糧食滿倉，一派豐收年景。

Qiansi Gate: No more existent, the Gate was at the joint point of the Yangtze and Jialing rivers, first recorded in writing as early as the Song Dynasty(960~1279). This used to be the berth area for the boats on the Jialing River, as well as the distributing center of traditional Chinese medicine, paper, salt and coal. The name Qiansi came from a famous ancient Chinese poem which means good harvest and prosperity.

《典藏重慶》系列攝影作品 (2) 重慶出版集团 重慶出版社
攝影編著：戴前鋒　翻譯：張兵一
SERIES PHOTO WORKS OF CHONGQING
PHOTOGRAPHER & COMPILER: DAI QIANFENG TRANSLATOR: ZHANG BINGYI

邮政编码 postcode

洪崖洞：位于嘉陵江畔，重慶古迹之一。舊時，夏秋有瀑布懸空，冬春有夕陽返照，五色陸離，時稱“洪崖滴翠”。

Hongyadong: One of the historic sites by the Jialing River. Many years back there was a waterfall in summer and autumn, and rainbow-like shine of the setting sun in winter and spring.

貼郵

stamp

《典藏重慶》系列攝影作品 (2) 重慶出版集团 重慶出版社
攝影編著：戴前鋒 翻譯：張兵一
SERIES PHOTO WORKS OF CHONGQING
PHOTOGRAPHER & COMPILER: DAI QIANFENG TRANSLATOR: ZHANG BINGYI

邮政编码 postcode

春至洪崖洞
Hongyadong in spring

貼郵
stamp

春至洪崖洞

Hongyadong in spring

洪崖洞：位于嘉陵江畔，重慶古迹之一。舊時，夏秋有瀑布懸空，冬春有夕陽返照，五色陸離，時稱“洪崖滴翠”。

Hongyadong: One of the historic sites by the Jialing River. Many years back there was a waterfall in summer and autumn, and rainbow-like shine of the setting sun in winter and spring.

《典藏重慶》系列攝影作品 (2) 重慶出版集团 重慶出版社
攝影編著：戴前鋒　翻譯：張兵一
SERIES PHOTO WORKS OF CHONGQING
PHOTOGRAPHER & COMPILER: DAI QIANFENG TRANSLATOR: ZHANG BINGYI

邮政编码 postcode

貼郵
stamp

紙鹽河巷：本名紙鹽河街，在千厮門外嘉陵江邊。此街内與城北垣外江平行，過去是紙碼頭、鹽碼頭，抗日戰争時期，紙碼頭、鹽碼頭、猪毛街、大火巷合并爲紙鹽河街。

Zhiyanhe Lane: This was a street by and along the Jialing River, once called Zhiyanhe Street. There used to be docks for paper and salt. During the Anti-Japanese War the paper dock, salt dock, Zhumao Street merged into the street of Zhiyanhe.

《典藏重慶》系列攝影作品 (2) 重慶出版集團 重慶出版社
攝影編著：戴前鋒　翻譯：張兵一
SERIES PHOTO WORKS OF CHONGQING
PHOTOGRAPHER & COMPILER: DAI QIANFENG TRANSLATOR: ZHANG BINGYI

邮政编码 postcode

貼郵
stamp

黃花園：原有黃花園街，中街在臨江門外北區路西段，富城路與大溪溝之間，北臨嘉陵江。昔有農民在這一帶種黃花得名。

Huanghuayuan: "Huanghua" meant "day lily", which was grown here by peasants. There used to be a Huanghuayuan Steet, the mid-part of which was the western part of Beiqu Road outside of Linjiang Gate, between Fucheng Road and Daxigou, with the Jialing River on its north side.

《典藏重慶》系列攝影作品（2） 重慶出版集團 重慶出版社
攝影編著：戴前鋒　翻譯：張兵一
SERIES PHOTO WORKS OF CHONGQING
PHOTOGRAPHER & COMPILER: DAI QIANFENG　TRANSLATOR: ZHANG BINGYI

邮政编码 postcode

貼郵
stamp

黄花園民居：原有黄花園街，中街在臨江門外北區路西段，富城路與大溪溝之間，北臨嘉陵江。昔有農民在這一帶種黄花得名。

Huanghuayuan: "Huanghua" meant "day lily", which was grown here by peasants. There used to be a Huanghuayuan Steet, the mid-part of which was the western part of Beiqu Road outside of Linjiang Gate, between Fucheng Road and Daxigou, with the Jialing River on its north side.

《典藏重慶》系列攝影作品 (2) 重慶出版集团 重慶出版社
攝影编著：戴前鋒　翻譯：張兵一
SERIES PHOTO WORKS OF CHONGQING
PHOTOGRAPHER & COMPILER: DAI QIANFENG TRANSLATOR: ZHANG BINGYI

邮政编码 postcode

貼郵
stamp

棉花街：是一條以行業命名的老街，曾是棉紗集中交易的市場。

Mianhua Street: "Mianhua" meant cotton in Chinese. The name came from the cotton yarn business in the street.

邮政编码 postcode

《典藏重慶》系列攝影作品 (2) 重慶出版集团 重慶出版社
攝影编著：戴前鋒　翻譯：張兵一
SERIES PHOTO WORKS OF CHONGQING
PHOTOGRAPHER & COMPILER: DAI QIANFENG TRANSLATOR: ZHANG BINGYI

保安路(現八一路)
Bao'an Road (now August 1st Road)

保安路（現八一路）：位于市中心，1939年被日機炸毁，重建后警察局駐此命名保安路。

Bao'an Road (now August 1st Road): Destroyed by Japanese bombardment in 1939, this road at downtown was rebuilt and named Bao'an (security) for the newly moved-in police station.

貼郵
stamp

《典藏重慶》系列攝影作品（2） 重慶出版集团 重慶出版社
攝影編著：戴前鋒　翻譯：張兵一
SERIES PHOTO WORKS OF CHONGQING
PHOTOGRAPHER & COMPILER: DAI QIANFENG TRANSLATOR: ZHANG BINGYI

邮政编码 postcode

民生美食城

□□□□□□

青年路：位于市中心，清末名爲天主教堂街。1939年“五三”、“五四”日機大轟炸毀壞，1944年重建，三民主義青年宫建于此（現實驗劇場），將此命名青年路。

Qingnian Road: Located in downtown, it was called Catholic Church Road during the late Qing Dynasty. The road was completely destroyed by Japanese bombardment on May 3rd and 4th, 1939, rebuilt in 1944 and then used as Youth Palace of the Three People's Principles. And its name was changed into Qingnian(youth) Road.

貼郵
stamp

《典藏重慶》系列攝影作品（2） 重慶出版集团 重慶出版社
攝影編著：戴前鋒　翻譯：張兵一
SERIES PHOTO WORKS OF CHONGQING
PHOTOGRAPHER & COMPILER: DAI QIANFENG TRANSLATOR: ZHANG BINGYI

邮政编码 postcode

三民主義青年宮（現實驗劇場）
Youth Palace of the Three People's Principles (now Shiyan Theatre)

貼郵
stamp

三民主義青年宫（現實驗劇場）：重慶三民主義青年團修建。1950年改爲實驗川劇院。

Youth Palace of the Three People's Principles (now Shiyan Theatre): It was built by Chongqing Youth League of the Three People's Principles and changed into a theatre in 1950.

《典藏重慶》系列攝影作品 (2) 重慶出版集团 重慶出版社
攝影編著：戴前鋒 翻譯：張兵一
SERIES PHOTO WORKS OF CHONGQING
PHOTOGRAPHER & COMPILER: DAI QIANFENG TRANSLATOR: ZHANG BINGYI

邮政编码 postcode

國民參政會舊址
The former site of the the National Consultation Council

貼郵
stamp

國民參政會舊址：位于中華路174號（原油市街4號），建于20世紀二三十年代，1938年7月國民參政會在武漢成立，同年遷重慶駐此辦公。

The former site of the the National Consultation Council: The house was built during the 1920s and 1930s at No.174, Zhonghua Road(the former No.4, Youshi Street). The National Consultation Council of the nationalist government was set up in July, 1938 in Wuhan and moved in here the same year.

《典藏重慶》系列攝影作品（2） 重慶出版集团 重慶出版社
攝影編著：戴前鋒　翻譯：張兵一
SERIES PHOTO WORKS OF CHONGQING
PHOTOGRAPHER & COMPILER: DAI QIANFENG TRANSLATOR: ZHANG BINGYI

邮政编码 postcode

小米市
Xiaomishi

58

貼郵
stamp

小米市：昔人稱關廟什字。因其長期是一個大米交易場所，也稱米亭子。重慶米糧業同業公會就在靠關廟街的一個大院內，米糧的大宗交易便在那裏面進行。
老房子後面的高建築爲新建的萬豪大酒店。

Xiaomishi: Formerly called Guanmiao Shizi, it got its name because of its rice market, so it was also called Mitingzi. Chongqing Rice Trade Society used to be in the large courtyard near Guanmiao Street, where bulk sales of rice were carried out.
The tall building at the background is Marriott Hotel.

《典藏重慶》系列攝影作品 (2) 重慶出版集团 重慶出版社
攝影編著：戴前鋒 翻譯：張兵一
SERIES PHOTO WORKS OF CHONGQING
PHOTOGRAPHER & COMPILER: DAI QIANFENG TRANSLATOR: ZHANG BINGYI

邮政编码 postcode

民國路（現五一路）
Minguo Road (now May 1st Road)

贴邮
stamp

民國路（現五一路）：位于市中心，1937年爲機房街，1939年被日機轟炸，1943年重建后命名爲民國路，“文革”中改名五一路。

Minguo Road (now May 1st Road): Located in downtown, the road was called Jifang Street in 1937, renamed in 1943 when it was rebuilt after its destruction by Japanese bombardment. May 1st Road was the name given to it during the Cultural Revolution.

《典藏重慶》系列攝影作品 (2) 重庆出版集团 重庆出版社
攝影編著：戴前鋒 翻譯：張兵一
SERIES PHOTO WORKS OF CHONGQING
PHOTOGRAPHER & COMPILER: DAI QIANFENG TRANSLATOR: ZHANG BINGYI

邮政编码 postcode

民生路至臨江路口

The crossing of Minsheng Road and Linjiang Road

貼郵
stamp

民生路至臨江路口：抗日戰争時期，重慶爲戰時首都，當時的美軍招待所就在此路。1945年抗戰勝利，改爲勝利大厦，1950年爲西南軍政委員會交際處第三招待所，1954年改爲重慶賓館。

The crossing of Minsheng Road and Linjiang Road: When Chongqing was the wartime capital of China during the Anti-Japanese War, this was the former site of the US Army guesthouse, which was renamed Building of Victory in 1945 when the war was won. In 1950 it became the guesthouse of the Social Activities Department of CPC Southwest Council of Military & Governmental Affairs, and in 1954 it was turned into Chongqing Guesthouse.

《典藏重慶》系列攝影作品（2） 重慶出版集团 重慶出版社
攝影編著：戴前鋒　翻譯：張兵一
SERIES PHOTO WORKS OF CHONGQING
PHOTOGRAPHER & COMPILER: DAI QIANFENG TRANSLATOR: ZHANG BINGYI

邮政编码 postcode

十八梯吊脚楼街市

The wooden-pillar-supported houses in Shibati

贴邮
stamp

十八梯吊脚樓街市

The wooden-pillar-supported houses in Shibati

十八梯：抗戰時，較場口連接下半城的石梯通道，在日機轟炸中，此處發生了震驚中外的大隧道慘案，死亡數千人。

Shibati: This was a long stone stairway connecting Jiaochangkou and the lower city, where thousands of people died of Japanese bombardment in and out of the tunnel in Shibati.

邮政编码 postcode

《典藏重慶》系列攝影作品（2） 重慶出版集团 重慶出版社
攝影編著：戴前鋒 翻譯：張兵一
SERIES PHOTO WORKS OF CHONGQING
PHOTOGRAPHER & COMPILER: DAI QIANFENG TRANSLATOR: ZHANG BINGYI

十八梯吊脚樓

The wooden-pillar-supported houses in Shibati

十八梯吊脚樓

The wooden-pillar-supported houses in Shibati

十八梯：抗戰時，較場口連接下半城的石梯通道，在日機轟炸中，此處發生了震驚中外的大隧道慘案，死亡數千人。

Shibati: This was a long stone stairway connecting Jiaochangkou and the lower city, where thousands of people died of Japanese bombardment in and out of the tunnel in Shibati.

貼郵
stamp

郵政编码 postcode

《典藏重慶》系列攝影作品（2） 重慶出版集团 重慶出版社
攝影編著：戴前鋒　翻譯：張兵一
SERIES PHOTO WORKS OF CHONGQING
PHOTOGRAPHER & COMPILER: DAI QIANFENG　TRANSLATOR: ZHANG BINGYI

贴邮
stamp

百子巷：此處小巷密布，故名百支巷，後取多子多福之意，更名百子巷。民國時期，巷內有川東師範學校、大生醫院、警士學校、儒善堂等。陪都時期，百子巷13號創辦了國際劇場，演出話劇、川劇等，是各業商販的聚集地。

Baizi Lane: The lane was first called Baizhi Lane because many small lanes gathered here. It was later changed into the present name, after the old saying of "more children and happier life". During the Republic of China, Eastern Sichuan Normal School, Dasheng Hospital, Police School, Rushan Charity House, etc. were located here. The International Theater was founded at No.13, Baizi Lane during the period of the War Capital, many plays and Sichuan Opera were shown. It was a place frequented by pedlars.

《典藏重慶》系列攝影作品 (2) 重慶出版集團 重慶出版社
攝影編著：戴前鋒　翻譯：張兵一
SERIES PHOTO WORKS OF CHONGQING
PHOTOGRAPHER & COMPILER: DAI QIANFENG TRANSLATOR: ZHANG BINGYI

邮政编码 postcode

唐式遵舊居

The former residence of Tang Shizun

貼郵
stamp

唐式遵舊居：位于金湯街80號，現九三學社重慶市委、中國民盟市委所在地。
唐式遵，抗戰期間任第三戰區副司令。

The former residence of Tang Shizun: Located at No. 80, Jintang Street, the house is now the office of Chongqing Committee of Jiusan Society and Chongqing Committee of China Democratic League.
Tang Shizun: Deputy Commander of the 3rd Theatre during the Anti-Japanese War.

《典藏重慶》系列攝影作品 (2) 重慶出版集团 重慶出版社
攝影編著：戴前鋒　翻譯：張兵一
SERIES PHOTO WORKS OF CHONGQING
PHOTOGRAPHER & COMPILER: DAI QIANFENG TRANSLATOR: ZHANG BINGYI

邮政编码 postcode

郭沫若舊居（天官府7號）
The former residence of Mr. Guo Moruo (No.7, Tianguan Mansion)

郭沫若舊居（天官府7號）：天官府，因明朝太師、吏部尚書（可稱天官）蹇義府第建于此得名。今渝中區天官府7號是抗日戰爭時期國民軍事委員會政治部第三廳和文化工作委員會的舊址。郭沫若時任“三廳”主任。此樓也曾爲重慶第一任市長潘文華的內務張營長的私宅。

The former residence of Mr. Guo Moruo (No.7, Tianguan Mansion): The place was named because it had been the location of residence of Jian Yi, Grand Mentor and Minister of Historiography of the Ming Dynasty. Located in now Yuzhong District, the residence is the former site of the Third Section of Department of Politics of KMT's Military Committee and Committee of Cultural Affairs during the Anti-Japanese War. Mr. Guo was the director of the Third Section. It had also been the private residence of Battalion Commander Zhang of Pan Wenhua, the first mayor of Chongqing.

貼郵
stamp

邮政编码 postcode

《典藏重慶》系列攝影作品 (2) 重慶出版集团 重慶出版社
攝影編著：戴前鋒 翻譯：張兵一
SERIES PHOTO WORKS OF CHONGQING
PHOTOGRAPHER & COMPILER: DAI QIANFENG TRANSLATOR: ZHANG BINGYI

思園
Siyuan

思園：位于民生路82號，臨街門面爲《新華日報》營業部舊址。

Siyuan: No.82, Minsheng Road. The house's facade to street used to be the business department of Xinhua Daily.

貼郵
stamp

《典藏重慶》系列攝影作品（2）重慶出版集團 重慶出版社
攝影編著：戴前鋒　翻譯：張兵一
SERIES PHOTO WORKS OF CHONGQING
PHOTOGRAPHER & COMPILER: DAI QIANFENG　TRANSLATOR: ZHANG BINGYI

邮政编码 postcode

韓國臨時政府舊址

The former site of the Provisional Government of the Republic of Korea

貼郵
stamp

韓國臨時政府舊址：位于今蓮花池38號。韓國臨時政府是一個長期在中國境内堅持反日獨立運動的流亡政府，1919年在上海成立，并制定了《大韓民國臨時章程》。抗戰爆發，隨國民政府西遷重慶。

The former site of the Provisional Government of the Republic of Korea: It was located at No.38, Lianhuachi. The Provisional Government of the Republic of Korea was established in Shanghai in 1919 and moved to Chongqing with the nationalist government after the breakout of the Anti-Japanese War. The provisional government persisted in anti-Japanese occupation and fought for Korea's independence in China, and drew up the Interim Regulations of the Repulic of Korea.

《典藏重慶》系列攝影作品 (2) 重慶出版集团 重慶出版社
攝影編著：戴前鋒　翻譯：張兵一
SERIES PHOTO WORKS OF CHONGQING
PHOTOGRAPHER & COMPILER: DAI QIANFENG TRANSLATOR: ZHANG BINGYI

邮政编码 postcode

保節院：保節院是慈善團體，于清光緒三年（公元1877年）普善堂道士楊季善購蓮花坊方家什字童姓房屋成立。此院給養節婦120名，由普善堂按月每人支銀1.5元。后遷往通遠門外，所在地以保節院命名，因有上保節院、下保節院，“文革”中改爲上三八街、下三八街、三八巷。院址在下三八街7號附14號，抗戰中被日機炸毀。

Baojieyuan: A charity organization started by Yang Jishan in 1877, it was first set up in a house Yang bought at Fangjia Shizi, Lianhuachi, before it was relocated to the outside of Tongyuan Gate, its name was kept for the place. The two places, the upper and the lower, were renamed the Upper Sanba （March 8th） Street and the Lower Sanba Street during the Cultural Revolution. The former site of Baojieyuan at No.7-14, the Lower Sanba Street, was destroyed by Japanese bombardment during the Anti-Japanese War.

貼郵
stamp

《典藏重慶》系列攝影作品（2） 重慶出版集团 重慶出版社
攝影編著：戴前鋒　翻譯：張兵一
SERIES PHOTO WORKS OF CHONGQING
PHOTOGRAPHER & COMPILER: DAI QIANFENG TRANSLATOR: ZHANG BINGYI

邮政编码 postcode

通遠門街市
The street market in Tongyuan Gate

貼郵
stamp

通遠門街市

The street market in Tongyuan Gate.

通遠門：是重慶十七城門中唯一接陸不臨水的開門之一。明洪武初在南宋故城舊址砌建，城門上書“克壯千秋”四字，月城城門北向。舊時去成都需出此門上東大道，故以“通向遠方的城門”之意得名。

Tongyuan Gate: Located at the western part of Yuzhong District, it was an open gate and the only one of the 17 gates in Chongqing that was built away from waters. It was built in 1368 on the remains of the ancient city of the Southern Song Dynasty, the gate of its satellite town facing north. Tongyuan literally means “toward far places” because it was the starting point of the major road to Chengdu.

《典藏重慶》系列攝影作品 (2) 重慶出版集团 重慶出版社
攝影編著：戴前鋒　翻譯：張兵一
SERIES PHOTO WORKS OF CHONGQING
PHOTOGRAPHER & COMPILER: DAI QIANFENG TRANSLATOR: ZHANG BINGYI

邮政编码 postcode

中山一路小巷

A small lane on No.1 Zhongshan Road

贴邮
stamp

中山一路小巷

A small lane on No.1 Zhongshan Road

中山路：重慶設市，開辟新市區，興修馬路，中區幹路從七星崗出城向西，經黃家埡口、觀音岩、上羅家灣，至兩路口轉北，經上清寺到曾家岩，抵嘉陵江邊。1937年全程建成后以中區幹路之意，分四段命名：中一路、中二路、中三路、中四路。抗戰爆發，國民政府移駐重慶，1937年爲紀念孫中山先生重新命名爲中山一路、中山二路、中山三路、中山四路。

Zhongshan Road: When Chongqing became a city from a town, a new downtown district was built, this road was among the many built with the district. The road started out of the city from Qixinggang to the west, led its way through Huangjiayakou, Guanyinyan, the Upper Luojiawan and turned north at Lianglukou, then it reached Shangqingsi and Zengjiayan, and finally the bank of the Jialing River. Finished in 1937, the main road was divided into four sections and named respectively as No.1 to No.4 Zhong Roads. After the relocation of the nationalist government in Chongqing, they were renamed as No.1 to No.4 Zhongshan Roads in memory of Sun Yat-sen (Sun Zhongshan).

《典藏重慶》系列攝影作品 (2) 重慶出版集团 重慶出版社
攝影編著：戴前鋒　翻譯：張兵一
SERIES PHOTO WORKS OF CHONGQING
PHOTOGRAPHER & COMPILER: DAI QIANFENG TRANSLATOR: ZHANG BINGYI

邮政编码 postcode

中山一路119號老宅

The old residence of No.119, No.1 Zhongshan Road

中山一路119號老宅

The old residence of No.119, No.1 Zhongshan Road

中山路：重慶設市，開辟新市區，興修馬路，中區幹路從七星崗出城向西，經黄家埡口、觀音岩、上羅家灣，至兩路口轉北，經上清寺到曾家岩，抵嘉陵江邊。1937年全程建成后以中區幹路之意，分四段命名：中一路、中二路、中三路、中四路。抗戰爆發，國民政府移駐重慶，1937年爲紀念孫中山先生重新命名爲中山一路、中山二路、中山三路、中山四路。

Zhongshan Road: When Chongqing became a city from a town, a new downtown district was built, this road was among the many built with the district. The road started out of the city from Qixinggang to the west, led its way through Huangjiayakou, Guanyinyan, the Upper Luojiawan and turned north at Lianglukou, then it reached Shangqingsi and Zengjiayan, and finally the bank of the Jialing River. Finished in 1937, the main road was divided into four sections and named respectively as No.1 to No.4 Zhong Roads. After the relocation of the nationalist government in Chongqing, they were renamed as No.1 to No.4 Zhongshan Roads in memory of Sun Yat-sen (Sun Zhongshan).

《典藏重慶》系列攝影作品（2） 重慶出版集团 重慶出版社

攝影編著：戴前鋒　翻譯：張兵一

SERIES PHOTO WORKS OF CHONGQING

PHOTOGRAPHER & COMPILER: DAI QIANFENG TRANSLATOR: ZHANG BINGYI

貼郵 stamp

邮政编码 postcode

歸元寺：位于通遠門外七星崗一帶山脊上，廟宇殘存，廟址今爲中一路小學及民居。中有寺內石門，門楣上題有“歸元禪林”、“覺路廣布”字樣。民居空地還有大覺和尚、嵩源和尚的塔（墓）。

Guiyuan Temple: The relics of the temple still remain on the ridge along Qixinggang, outside of Tongyuan Gate. On its site now are the No.1 Zhongshan Road Primary School and residential houses. The inscribed stone gate within the temple and the tower tombs of monks are still found on the site.

貼郵
stamp

《典藏重慶》系列攝影作品（2） 重慶出版集团 重慶出版社
攝影編著：戴前鋒　翻譯：張兵一
SERIES PHOTO WORKS OF CHONGQING
PHOTOGRAPHER & COMPILER: DAI QIANFENG TRANSLATOR: ZHANG BINGYI

邮政编码 postcode

中蘇文化協會舊址

The former site of Sino-Soviet Cultural Association

中蘇文化協會舊址：位于中山一路162號（原198號）。中蘇文化協會最初由國民政府立法委員張西曼領銜，同一些留蘇人士發起，1936年在南京成立，會長孫科，副會長陳立夫、邵力子。“抗戰”爆發后，1937年12月1日隨國民政府遷至重慶。協會有機關刊物《中蘇文化》。1946年隨國民政府還都南京。

The former site of Sino-Soviet Cultural Association: It was located at No.162 (formerly No.198), No.1 Zhongshan Road. Headed by Zhang Ximan, member of Legislation Committee of the nationalist government, those people back from their study in the Soviet Union initiated the founding of the association. It was founded in Nanjing in 1936, with Sun Ke as president, Chen Lifu and Shao Lizi as vice presidents. The association was relocated to Chongqing with the government on December 1st, 1937. It published a magazine called *Sino-Soviet Culture*. In 1940 it was reorganized for expansion, setting up under it several committees respectively of research, editting, translation, woman affairs and finance. Actually it was used as the place of activities by the Southern Bureau of CPC Central Committee. In 1946 the association moved back to Nanjing with the government.

《典藏重慶》系列攝影作品（2） 重慶出版集團 重慶出版社
攝影編著：戴前鋒　翻譯：張兵一
SERIES PHOTO WORKS OF CHONGQING
PHOTOGRAPHER & COMPILER: DAI QIANFENG TRANSLATOR: ZHANG BINGYI

貼郵
stamp

邮政编码 postcode

貼郵
stamp

蘇聯大使館：位于枇杷山正街104號（現重慶第三人民醫院辦公樓），由川軍師長曾子唯始建于1936年。大使館于1938年1月入駐，至1946年5月，其間爲避日機轟炸曾遷駐重慶南山鄉82號。

The USSR Embassy: Located at No.104, Pipashan Zhengjie—the present office building of Chongqing No.3 People's Hospital, the building had been built in 1936 by Zeng Ziwei, a divisional commander of the Sichuan Army before it was used as the embassy of the Soviet Union from January 1938 to May 1946, during which the embassy was once relocated to No.82, Nanshanxiang, because of the Japanese bombardment.

《典藏重慶》系列攝影作品（2） 重慶出版集团 重慶出版社
攝影編著：戴前鋒　翻譯：張兵一
SERIES PHOTO WORKS OF CHONGQING
PHOTOGRAPHER & COMPILER: DAI QIANFENG TRANSLATOR: ZHANG BINGYI

邮政编码 postcode

陳誠舊居
The former residence of Chen Cheng

75

陳誠舊居：位于渝中區勝利路187號現中國科技情報研究所重慶分所内，現爲職工宿舍。
陳誠（1897–1965），浙江青田縣人，保定軍官學校畢業。“抗戰”時期歷任第九、第六、第七戰區司令長官、軍委會政治部長、三青團書記長、遠徵軍司令長官、湖北省主席等職。授陸軍上將銜。

The former residence of Chen Cheng: Located at No.187, Shengli Road, Yuzhong District, the site is now within the courtyard of Chongqing Sub-Institute of Institute of Scientific & Technical Information of China, the former house is now the living quarters of the institute.
Chen Cheng (1897-1965), born in Qingtian County, Zhejiang Province, was the graduate of Baoding Army Officer School. During the Anti-Japanese War he was, successively, Commander-in-Chief of the 9th, 6th and 7th theatres, Minister of Politics of Military Committee, Secretary General of Sanqing League, Commander-in-Chief of China Expedition Army and Chairman of Hubei Province. During the civil war between the KMT and CPC, he was the Chief of the General Staff, Army General.

《典藏重慶》系列攝影作品（2） 重慶出版集團 重慶出版社
攝影編著：戴前鋒　翻譯：張兵一
SERIES PHOTO WORKS OF CHONGQING
PHOTOGRAPHER & COMPILER: DAI QIANFENG TRANSLATOR: ZHANG BINGYI

貼郵
stamp

邮政编码 postcode

勝利路民居
The residence on Shengli Road

勝利路民居：取抗戰勝利之意命名。

The residence on Shengli Road(Victory Road, for the celebration of the victory of the Anti-Japanese War).

貼郵
stamp

《典藏重慶》系列攝影作品 (2) 重慶出版集团 重慶出版社
攝影編著：戴前鋒 翻譯：張兵一
SERIES PHOTO WORKS OF CHONGQING
PHOTOGRAPHER & COMPILER: DAI QIANFENG TRANSLATOR: ZHANG BINGYI

邮政编码 postcode

抗戰勝利記功碑 77
The Monument to the Victory of the Anti-Japanese War

贴邮
stamp

抗戰勝利記功碑：位于渝中區民族路、民權路、鄒容路交會處。1941年爲了動員全民抗戰，在原址上建有象徵民族精神的木質建築“精神堡壘”。抗戰勝利後，社會各界曾提議在此塑一蔣中正銅像，被蔣介石斷然否決。1947年，抗戰勝利記功碑在此落成。碑座立面刻有定都重慶全文，張群、吳鼎昌、張篤倫分别撰寫碑文，重慶市參議會題詞，美國總統羅斯福贈重慶市民的卷軸譯文等。

The Monument to the Victory of the Anti-Japanese War: Located at the junction of Minzu Road, Minquan Road and Zourong Road, Yuzhong District, it used to be a wooden monument first built In 1941, originally called Spiritual Fortress, for mobilizing an "allround anti-Japanese war". After the victory of the war, the social circles of Chongqing suggested to build a bronze statue of Chiang Kai-shek on the site, which was turned down by Chiang. In 1947 the The Monument to the Victory of the Anti-Japanese War was built on the site of the Spiritual Fortress, on which inscribed the full text of Declaration of Relocation of the Nationalist Government to Chongqing, the articles written by Zhang Qun, Wu Dingchang and Zhang Dulun, as well as the inscription by Chongqing Consultation Council and the Chinese translation of the text on the scroll presented to Chongqing people by President Franklin Delano Roosevelt.

《典藏重慶》系列攝影作品 (2) 重慶出版集团 重慶出版社
攝影編著：戴前鋒　翻譯：張兵一
SERIES PHOTO WORKS OF CHONGQING
PHOTOGRAPHER & COMPILER: DAI QIANFENG TRANSLATOR: ZHANG BINGYI

邮政编码 postcode